THE LEARNING WORKS SCIENCE SERIES

BIRDS

Written and Illustrated by Beverly Armstrong

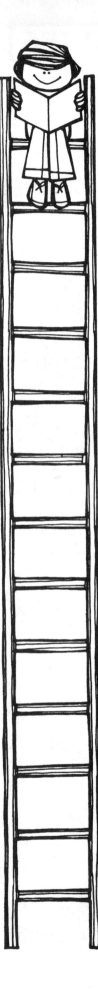

The Learning Works

Edited by Sherri M. Butterfield

The purchase of this book entitles the individual classroom teacher to reproduce copies for use in the classroom.

The reproduction of any part for an entire school or school system or for commercial use is strictly prohibited.

No form of this work may be reproduced or transmitted or recorded without written permission from the publisher.

Contents

BIRDS © 1988—The Learning Works, Inc.

Brown Pelican

In coastal areas of the Americas, the brown pelican may be seen slowly gliding through the air and then suddenly dropping headfirst into the ocean to catch fish. As this master diver moves through the water, the pouch on the underside of its bill expands to become a huge scoop that can hold more than a gallon of water—and fish!

Brown pelicans prefer to stay near shore. They live in flocks of up to fifty birds and build nests that are little more than bulky piles of sticks. Young pelicans thrust their heads deep into their parents' pouches to eat. These strange-looking chicks grow quickly and have been known to outweigh their parents before they become independent.

During the 1970s, the insecticide DDT caused pelicans to lay thin-shelled eggs, which broke before hatching. As a result, the number of brown pelicans dwindled, and this species became seriously endangered. Laws prohibiting the use of DDT have enabled the brown pelican to make a comeback.

Coloring Clues

This bird is grayish-brown with white markings on its face and neck. The back of its neck is reddish-brown. The brown pelican's blue eyes are surrounded by pink skin. Its bill, pouch, and feet are yellow.

Activity Safari

1. Litter, such as discarded nets, lengths of fishing line, and plastic six-pack holders, can prove deadly to sea birds. The birds get their beaks, feet, necks, or wings entangled in these items and may become crippled, strangled, or starved. Design a poster to inform people about the threat posed by carelessly discarded litter to the brown pelican and other waterfowl.

2. The pelican's webbed feet make it an excellent swimmer. Name five other birds that have webbed feet.

Brown Pelican (*Pelecanus occidentalus*)

Burrowing Owl

These small owls are found in the grasslands and semideserts of North, Central, and South America. They live in burrows that they have dug or in the abandoned homes of animals such as badgers, prairie dogs, and tortoises. Burrowing owls are active during the day. They eat insects, lizards, mice, and other small animals. Their range is being reduced by the spread of agriculture. Plowing destroys their burrows, and these owls often die after eating insects and rodents that have been poisoned by farmers.

Coloring Clues

Burrowing owls are brown and white. They have white "eyebrows," yellow eyes, and brown facial discs (feathers around the eyes). The beak and legs are tan.

Activity Safari

1. Imagine that you want to protect land that houses a burrowing owl colony from being used for agriculture. Design a flier encouraging others to support this project. In your flier, explain the importance of saving these owls and tell how donated money will be spent.

2. Burrowing owls help control destructive insects and rodents. If an owl caught seven grasshoppers each day and three mice each week for eight weeks, what would be the total numbers of grasshoppers and mice caught?

3. Make a burrowing owl colony to hang in your room. Decorate small brown paper bags to look like owls. Add construction paper legs. Hang the owls from a coat hanger, dowel, or branch.

BIRDS © 1988—The Learning Works, Inc.

Burrowing Owl (*Athene cunicularia*)

Gold and Blue Macaw

Macaws are the largest of the parrots, and this bird is the second largest of the macaws. It is three feet long from beak to tail tip. Gold and blue macaws fly through South American jungles in vast screeching flocks, feeding on fruits, nuts, and seeds. Their powerful beaks and strong grasping feet are useful for collecting food. In February, these parrots nest in hollow trees, where the males feed the females and the females feed the chicks.

For centuries, macaws have been hunted for their feathers. As a result, several species have become extinct. More recently, the popularity of parrots as pets has led to the deaths of thousands of macaws. Hunters kill parent birds to collect their chicks, and many young birds die because they are kept in crowded cages with poor ventilation and inadequate nourishment while they are being illegally smuggled out of one country and into another.

Coloring Clues

The chest, eyes, and lower tail feathers of this macaw are golden yellow. Its forehead is green. The back, wings, and top tail feathers are blue. The face is white, and the chin feathers and beak are black.

Activity Safari

1. Most young animals grow and mature more rapidly than human babies. For example, when young macaws are six months old, they are as large as their parents. At approximately what age do human children reach adult size?

2. Compare the size, appearance, and contents of the macaw's jungle habitat with a well-furnished parrot cage. In what ways are they similar? In what ways are they different? How would you feel about living in a cage the size of a telephone booth or elevator? Which of the activities that you now enjoy would be impossible in so small a space? Express your thoughts in a paragraph or poem.

BIRDS © 1988—The Learning Works, Inc.

Gold and Blue Macaw (*Ara ararauna*)

Great Blue Heron

The great blue heron—a four-foot-tall bird—stalks through reedy swamps and streams, spearing fish, frogs, and other water animals with its knifelike bill. It also hunts mice and gophers in meadows. Herons often nest in noisy treetop colonies and fly twenty or thirty miles to feeding grounds. Their nests are large platforms made from sticks. In spring, the female great blue heron lays three to six blue-green eggs, which are incubated by both parents. The young grow quickly, staying in the nest until their feathers develop and then teetering on branches as they watch eagerly for their parents to bring food. At summer's end, the young herons become independent.

Coloring Clues

This bird is bluish-gray with a brownish-gray neck. Its eyes, bill, and legs are yellow. It has white markings on its face and black areas on its head, wings, and belly.

Activity Safari

1. Compare this heron's four-foot height with your own.

2. The English word **heron** comes from the Old French word *hairon.* Below are the Old English names for some common birds. Can you identify them?

   cran   cycen   finc   gos   storc   wrenna

3. Many bird identification books contain descriptions of the sounds made by different types of birds. Find a bird book and try to make some of the sounds that it describes. Here are a few to get you started.

great blue heron	CRAAACK!
acorn woodpecker	Wake up, wake up, wake up.
herring gull	Keeyah, keeyah!

Great Blue Heron (*Ardea herodias*)

Great Hornbill

Great hornbills honk and flap their way through Asian jungles in small flocks. With their huge beaks, they snatch and gobble fruit, insects, snakes, and centipedes. The beak, with its crestlike casque, is strong but lightweight. These five-foot-long birds have strong wings, short legs, and long flapping tails.

Great hornbills have unusual nesting habits. The female climbs into a hollow tree and plasters the entrance closed with her droppings, leaving only a small slit, which is just wide enough for the male's beak. While she raises the young in this safe chamber, he feeds the family. Eventually, the female and babies break out and fly away.

Coloring Clues

This hornbill has pale blue eyes surrounded by bright red skin. Its beak and casque are yellow. Its body and face are black, and the latter is framed by a mane of fine yellow feathers.

Activity Safari

1. The world's rain forests, home for hornbills and thousands of other unique animals, are being destroyed by people at the rate of six thousand acres every hour. At this alarming rate, how many acres are destroyed in a twenty-four-hour period? How many are destroyed in a week?

2. The hornbill uses its beak to peel fruit, carry food, catch snakes and scorpions, play with twigs, and feed its chicks. Draw a picture of a hornbill that is doing one of these things.

3. Hornbills are noisy. They communicate with roaring, grunting, whistling, and laughing sounds. Make some hornbill noises while holding a cardboard tube (representing the bird's beak) in front of your mouth.

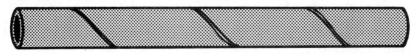

Great Hornbill (*Buceros bicornis*)

Greater Flamingo

Standing four feet tall, the greater flamingo is the largest and the most widespread of the flamingos. It lives in shallow, salty lakes and lagoons in parts of the Americas, southern Europe, Africa, and India. Hanging its head upside down underwater, the flamingo sweeps its strangely bent bill through the mud, filtering out snails, shrimp, and other small animals. Flamingos are strong fliers and can swim well. When resting, they usually stand on one leg, folding their long necks over their backs. Thousands of flamingos may live in a single colony. Pairs of birds work together to build chimney-like nests of mud and sand. When a nest is completed, the female lays a single white egg atop it.

Coloring Clues

The body, bill, and legs of this flamingo may be any shade of pink. The eyes are yellow. The tips of both the bill and the wings are black.

Activity Safari

1. Create a poster encouraging people to visit the flamingo exhibit at a zoo. You may also want to design a bumper sticker, lapel button, or T-shirt promoting this exhibit.

2. A flamingo may eat a tenth of its body weight in food each day. If you were to eat a tenth of your weight, how many pounds of food would you consume?

3. An old legend says that, many years ago, when all of the animals were being assigned to their homes, the flamingos happened to be last in line. When their turn came, the only habitat left was a hot, smelly, saltwater lagoon. To compensate them for living in such an undesirable place, flamingos were given feathers the color of the sunrise. Make up a legend to explain the appearance of one of the other birds in this book.

Greater Flamingo (Phoenicopterus ruber)

Indian Peafowl

Egyptian royalty kept Indian peafowl as pets three thousand years ago. These members of the pheasant family adapt easily to life in captivity; and their shimmering beauty adds elegance to estates, gardens, and parks. In the wild, peafowl prefer grasslands with scattered trees and shrubs in which to roost at night. The male, or peacock, spreads the two hundred plumes of his magnificent train to attract the smaller, plainer peahen. She raises the young in a shallow nest-bowl scratched in the dirt, guarding them carefully and feeding them from her beak.

Coloring Clues

The peacock has a blue-green head and chest with white face markings. The scalelike feathers in front of its tail are yellow-green or gold. The "eyes" of its tail feathers are blue-green with black centers and rest on a gold background that is edged with yellow.

Activity Safari

1. The peacock is the national bird of India. The national bird of the United States is the bald eagle. Can you name the state bird of the state in which you live? If not, look it up in an encyclopedia under the name of your state.

2. When fully spread, the peacock's tail is nine feet wide. Cut a piece of string nine feet long and compare its length with the dimensions of objects in your house or yard.

3. Some residents of rural canyons in California keep peafowl to kill local rattlesnakes. Other canyon residents complain that the birds are both noisy and messy. These disgruntled neighbors want to make it illegal for people to keep peafowl as pets. How do you feel about this issue?

Indian Peafowl (*Pavo cristatus*)

King Bird of Paradise

Not much is known about these tiny, rare birds. They live deep in the forests of New Guinea, and their nests are rarely found. As with most birds of paradise, the females are pale brown, while the males are clad in strangely shaped feathers and dazzling colors. Several times a day, the males court the females by singing, swaying, and hanging upside down. King birds of paradise feed on fruits, insects, seeds, and small animals. Natives of New Guinea shoot birds of paradise with blowguns and collect their feathers to wear as ornaments. For this reason, several species have become extinct.

Coloring Clues

The male king bird of paradise, shown here, has a bright red head, neck, and back. Its eyes are gold, and its legs are blue. Its tail feathers are green, and there is a green stripe across its white chest. The "fans" on either side of its body are tan with white stripes and green edges.

Activity Safari

1. The king bird of paradise is **omnivorous.** If you do not know the meaning of this word, look it up. You may also want to look up these related words: **carnivorous, frugivorous, herbivorous,** and **insectivorous.**

2. Most of the forty different birds of paradise are brightly colored and have unusual tail feathers. They also have exotic names, such as King of Saxony and Princess Stephanie. Draw an imaginary bird of paradise and give it an exotic name.

3. The king bird of paradise lives in New Guinea. Find this island in an atlas or on a world map or globe. Is it north or south of the equator? To which country or countries does it belong?

King Bird of Paradise (*Cicinnurus regius*)

Lady Amherst Pheasant

The Lady Amherst pheasant is found in the high mountains of Tibet, Burma, and southwestern China. This spectacular bird prefers to live in woodlands and rocky areas, and needs safe places in which to roost at night. The brightly colored male must be especially watchful to avoid predators. Like chickens, these pheasants scratch the earth with their strong feet to dig up the insects and seeds on which they feed. The female scoops out a shallow nest, incubates her eggs, and raises the young with no help from her mate.

Coloring Clues

The male bird has a white beak, eyes, and chest feathers. His facial skin is blue, and he has a crest of thin red feathers. There are black-edged white feathers on the back of his neck, and black feathers on his throat. The top of this bird's back is gold; the lower third is red. The wings are glossy black. The long tail feathers are tan. Small orange feathers stick out on either side of the middle tail feather. The less colorful female pheasant is brown with black markings.

Activity Safari

1. Locate Burma, China, and Tibet on a map. The tallest mountain in the world is on the border between Tibet and Nepal. What is the name of this majestic peak? How tall is it?

2. In many bird species, the females are less colorful than the males. Drab coloring makes the females harder to see when they are sitting on their nests or caring for their young. Among which of the bird species listed below are the males and females similar in coloring? Among which species are they different? Use a bird book if you need help in answering these questions.

Canada goose	meadowlark
cardinal	mockingbird
mallard duck	red-winged blackbird

BIRDS © 1988—The Learning Works, Inc.

Lady Amherst Pheasant (*Chrysolophus amherstiae*)

Roadrunner

The roadrunner trots through deserts of the southwestern United States and Mexico, pursuing the insects, reptiles, and rodents that it eats. This curious, agile bird can run as fast as a person and can outmaneuver a coyote. The roadrunner's eyes operate independently. One eye can look forward, watching for prey, while the other eye looks up, scanning the sky for predators. The roadrunner makes a variety of cackling, clicking, and cooing sounds. Female roadrunners build messy nests of sticks and snakeskins in spiny desert plants.

Coloring Clues

The roadrunner's head, back, and tail are dark brown. The feathers on its wings have tan edges. Underneath, the bird is tan with streaks of brown. Its beak and legs are gray, and its eyes are yellow. The bare strip of skin behind each eye is blue near the eye and red farther back.

Activity Safari

1. A roadrunner can run at the rate of twenty-six miles per hour. Make a bar graph comparing the roadrunner's speed with the animal speeds listed below.

bee	11 mph	elephant	25 mph
chicken	9 mph	giraffe	31 mph
dolphin	36 mph	lobster	17 mph

2. Roadrunners have **zygodactyl** feet. Find this word in a big dictionary. What does it mean?

3. The roadrunner has black skin. On cold mornings, it raises its feathers so that the sun can shine directly on its skin. To find out how the roadrunner's dark-colored skin helps warm the bird, set pieces of dark- and light-colored paper or clothing out in the sun. After ten minutes, feel these items. Which one absorbed more warmth, the dark one or the light one? Why?

Roadrunner (*Geococcyx californianus*)

Rockhopper Penguin

These small, crested penguins live in huge, noisy colonies in the Falklands and other islands around Antarctica. With their sharp-clawed feet, they scramble over boulders and tussock grasses from the colony to the sea. After diving into the water, they "fly" swiftly and gracefully through the waves, snapping up fish and shrimplike krill with their strong beaks. The penguins then return to the colony's nursery to feed their fluffy, waddling youngsters. Pollution of the ocean is a threat to these birds.

Coloring Clues

The black-and-white rockhopper penguin has red-orange eyes, beak, and feet. Its shaggy "eyebrows" are yellow.

Activity Safari

1. Colonies of rockhopper penguins are found on several islands around Antarctica. On a map of the Antarctic, locate these islands, which are inhabited by rockhoppers.

Falkland Islands	New Amsterdam
Tristan da Cunha	Saint Paul
Gough	Bounty Islands

2. Make a "penguin pole" to show the relative sizes of these birds. Tape a four-inch-by-four-foot strip of paper to a wall so that one end touches the floor. Use a pencil and ruler to mark the heights of these penguin species on the strip. All measurements are in inches.

Chinstrap	27	Humboldt	26
Emperor	45	King	37
Galapagos	21	Little Blue	15½
Gentoo	32	Macaroni	28
	Rockhopper	22	

Rockhopper Penguin *(Eudyptes crestatus)*

Tawny Frogmouth

The tawny frogmouth is a strange woodland bird of Australia and Tasmania. During the daytime, it disguises itself as a dead branch, stretching upward and remaining motionless. At night, it perches in low trees and pounces silently down onto insects, reptiles, and other animals passing below. It snatches, pounds, and swallows these hapless creatures with its huge, wide bill. When confronted by enemies, the frogmouth puffs up its feathers and glares fiercely, trying to scare them away.

Coloring Clues

The tawny frogmouth is mottled reddish-brown or gray. Its beak is tan, and its eyes are bright yellow.

Activity Safari

1. Frogmouths may be either gray or brown. Animals such as this, which naturally come in two different color "phases," are called **dichromatic.** The screech owl is dichromatic. Look for pictures of its two phases in a bird book.

2. The name **frogmouth** describes this bird's wide bill. Can you think of descriptive names for the imaginary animals listed below?

   a mouse with a very long, thin tail
   a lizard with sharp, spiny scales
   a goose with very wide feet

3. Frogmouth eggs hatch thirty days after they are laid. Make a time line comparing this incubation period with the others listed below. The numbers specify days.

bald eagle	35	ostrich	42
black swan	38	roadrunner	18
canary	14	spoonbill	21

Tawny Frogmouth (*Podargus strigoides*)

Wood Duck

Wood ducks are found near ponds, streams, and swamps in wooded areas of the United States and southwestern Canada. Their short wings and sharp-clawed feet enable them to fly between forest trees and to climb among branches. Wood ducks nest in holes in dead trees. Because their nests may be as much as fifty feet above ground and a mile from water, newly hatched ducklings must make wild leaps as they follow their mothers for the first time. Wood ducks eat acorns, insects, minnows, snails, and water plants. The males of this species are brightly colored while the females are mostly brown.

Coloring Clues

The male wood duck has an orange beak with a yellow stripe at its base. His eyes are red, and his glossy head feathers are dark green, purple, or black. There are white stripes on his head and under his chin. His chest is rust-colored with white spots, and his sides are gold. Black and white stripes separate his sides from his chest and back. His back is rust-colored, and his wing feathers are dark blue.

Activity Safari

1. This bird is also known as the Carolina duck, the summer duck, and the tree duck because of its habitat and habits. Can you think of at least one animal whose name begins with each of these adjectives?

     black   king   sand   sea   water   wood

2. Ducks are **precocial.** When the babies hatch, they are covered with down. Within an hour, they can walk and feed themselves. In what ways do the babies of **altricial** birds, such as sparrows and robins, differ from the babies of precocial birds, such as baby ducks?

3. The wood duck is closely related to the beautiful mandarin duck of China and Japan. Look for a picture of this unusual bird in a bird book or an encyclopedia.

Wood Duck (*Aix sponsa*)

Zebra Finch

Many flocks of zebra finches flutter through Australia's grasslands and savannahs. These perky little birds are bold and curious among people, and are commonly kept as pets in the United States. Zebra finches eat grass seeds and small insects. They build untidy nests and breed almost year-round. The black beaks of young zebra finches turn red when these birds reach maturity. Parent finches feed their young as long as their beaks are black but stop doing so as soon as they change color.

Coloring Clues

Zebra finches have red beaks and legs. The female is gray-brown above with a lighter chest and black and white facial markings. The male has a gray-brown back and head. His cheeks are orange, and his sides are rust-brown with white spots. His light-gray chest has black markings, and his tail is black and white.

Activity Safari

1. Zebra finches build their nests from feathers, grass, roots, twigs, and wool or other animal hair. Gather some of these materials and try to weave them into a nest.

2. Occasionally, zebra finches and other birds reuse old, abandoned nests instead of building new ones. For this reason, it is not a good idea for people to collect birds' nests. Design a poster that encourages people to leave nests alone.

3. Many finches have interesting and descriptive names. Use some of the finch names listed below to make a word search puzzle.

cherry	red ear
cutthroat	shafttail
fire	silverbill
lavender	spice
owl	star
painted	strawberry

Zebra Finch (*Taeniopygia castanotis*)

Bird Facts

The largest bird is the North African ostrich, which may stand more than eight feet tall and weigh almost three hundred and fifty pounds.

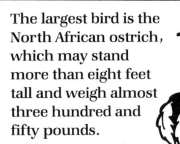

Tailorbirds build nests between large leaves which they have sewn together.

Mockingbirds imitate the sounds of human voices and machines as well as the calls of other birds.

The spoonbill catches small water animals with its long beak.

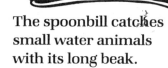

Hummingbirds can fly backwards.

Parrots and cockatoos often live for more than fifty years.

Arctic terns may fly 24,000 miles in a year.

The wrybill's strange beak twists to the right.

The wandering albatross may have a wingspan of more than eleven feet.

Peregrine falcons dive at speeds up to 150 miles per hour.

The chicken-sized kiwi lays an egg that is five inches long and weighs one pound.

The tail feathers of an onagadori rooster may be more than thirty-four feet long.

Woodpecker finches use cactus spines to catch insects hiding in small holes or crevices.

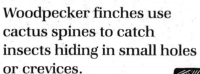

Birds of prey can see eight to ten times better than people can.

The bee hummingbird is 2¼ inches long, including its beak and its tail. It weighs a little more than half an ounce.